GRADE 3 WORKBOOK

Table of Contents

by Sarah J. Carroll

Editor
Lisa Penttilä

Layout & Design
Michael P. Brodey

This Grade 3 edition published
by Telegraph Road
36 Northline Road,
Toronto, Ontario, Canada
M4B 3E2

ALL RIGHTS RESERVED
ISBN: 978-177062076-6

For special bulk purchases please contact:
sales@telegraph-rd.com

For other inquiries please contact:
inquiries@telegraph-rd.com

Printed in China

Dear Parents,

Welcome to the Giant Grade 3 Workbook! Every page is chock full of exercises, games, and puzzles that reinforce the main concepts taught in Grade 3 plus colourful illustrations that stimulate a sense of fun.

The activities provide language and math curriculum practice that can be used during the school year to reinforce school learning, as summer preparation for an upcoming gra... ...review between grades.

By the end of Grade 3, student... ...monstrate an understanding of a variety ... ...ds and cueing systems to read fluentl...  ...e and order numbers to 1000, add a... ...multiply one-digit numbers, and calcula... ...They build on skills they have developed in Grade 2 an... ...junior division when they enter Grade 4.

Practice is essential in helping students become confident learners, but remember that all children learn at their own rate. The exercises have been ordered to help children build on skills previously introduced; however many children may wish to complete the book in a different order.

In the math section, you will find explanations that will help familiarize you with some of the current terminology used in schools. For example, in the addition and subtraction section, the term 're-grouping' (which has replaced 'borrowing,' a change that often causes confusion between parents and children) is demonstrated for the benefit of the student and the parent.

Parents, the activities in this book will challenge your Grade 3 children and provide them with important practice, while the mixture of imaginative activities means they'll have fun completing every page!

Finally a big thank you to the kids who field-tested the workbook: Samantha Casey, Corrina Malfatti, Kaylin Miller and Matthew Proctor.

Sincerely,

Sarah J. Carroll

Sarah J. Carroll, M.A., B.Ed.

We can show a number using base ten blocks.

= 1 | = 10   = 100   = 1000

Here are three ways to show a number:

Model with base ten blocks	Numerals and words	Expanded form
+ +	1 thousand + 2 hundreds + 3 tens + 4 ones	1000 + 200 + 30 + 4
= 1,234	= 1,234	= 1,234

Fill in the blanks to show two ways to show the number 1,346.

1. Base ten block model

2. Numerals and words

How many thousands? ⬇ ☐

How many hundreds? ⬇ ☐

How many tens? ⬇ ☐

How many ones? ⬇ ☐

3. Write in expanded form

⬇ _____ + ⬇ _____ + ⬇ _____ + ⬇ _____

Fill in the blanks.

How many thousands?	How many hundreds?	How many tens?	How many ones?	
				= ☐ TOTAL

How many thousands?	How many hundreds?	How many tens?	How many ones?	
				= ☐ TOTAL

How many thousands?	How many hundreds?	How many tens?	How many ones?	
				= ☐ TOTAL

Place Value

Hey-Kids!

Sketch the base ten blocks like this.

Expanded form is a way of showing the value of each digit. For example, 731 in expanded form is 700+30+1.

	Numeral	Numerals and Words	Sketch of base 10 blocks
1.	19	1 ten + 9 ones	
2.	7		
3.	22		
4.	113		
5.	693		
6.	376		
7.	264		
8.	251		
9.	428		
10.	13		

Write each number in expanded form.

11.	193	100+90+3
12.	323	
13.	478	
14.	99	
15.	619	
16.	765	
17.	567	
18.	130	
19.	943	
20.	286	
21.	658	
22.	444	
23.	337	
24.	786	
25.	86	
26.	962	
27.	10	
28.	111	
29.	59	
30.	63	

Skip Counting

Fill in the *blanks* from cloud to cloud to complete the path.

150   152   159   165   170   175
151

Try skip counting by 5 to help the frog leap across the lily pads.

75   80   95   100   105   120   135

Skip count by 3s. Fill in the numbers on the blank boards to complete the bridge. Don't fall into the water!

3   6   9   21   36   48   60

Skip count by 2s. Fill in the blanks on the rocks.

32   34   44   4   54

by 10
0
20
60
100

Skip count by 25
0
25
200

Addition without regrouping

When we add, we find the **sum**. First we add the ones, then the tens, and then the hundreds.

Add the ones:	Next add the tens:	Next add the hundreds:

```
  3 2|5|        3|2|5         |3|2 5
+ 2 6|1|      + 2|6|1       + |2|6 1
  ---|-|        -|-|-         |-|---
     |6|         |8|6         |5|8 6
```

Try these.

```
  1 2 6         4 6          6 8
+ 3 5 2       + 3 3        + 2 1
---------     -------      -------
```

```
  3 1 1         1 3 2        6 3 1
+ 4 6 7       + 2 2 5      + 3 2 4
---------     ---------    ---------
```

Addition with regrouping

When the sum in any column is greater than 9, we need to regroup that number. See how this works in this example:

```
  1
  7|8|
+ 5|6|
  -|-|
   |4|
```
We add the ones column, 8+4=14. Since 14 is greater than 9, we have to regroup it into 1 ten and 4 ones. We put the 4 ones into the ones place and the 1 ten into the tens place.

```
 |1|
 |7|8
+|5|6
 |-|-
 |3|4
```
Now we add the tens, 1+7+5=13. We have to regroup the 13 tens into 1 hundred and 3 tens. We put the 3 tens into the tens place and the 1 hundred into the hundreds place.

```
|1|1
|  |7 8
+ |5 6
|-|---
|1|3 4
```
Finally we add the hundreds. 1+0=1. We have found the sum, 134.

Hint: Be sure to keep the numbers lined up in the right place value column.

Try these.

```
  2 5          2 6          1 5 6        8 1 6
+ 3 6        + 4 8        + 2 7        + 1 5 9
-------      -------      ---------    ---------
```

```
  7 8          7 1          3 2 1        2 6 7
+ 1 5        + 1 9        + 8 8        + 2 4 7
-------      -------      ---------    ---------
```

```
  4 3          8 4          4 7 7        6 9 9
+ 4 8        + 1 7        + 1 8 3      + 1 2 8
-------      -------      ---------    ---------
```

```
  7 5          3 7          7 6 5        5 7 5
+ 2 5        + 5 7        + 4 7 6      + 4 2 6
-------      -------      ---------    ---------
```

Addition Facts

Complete these addition facts and sail your way to the next page.

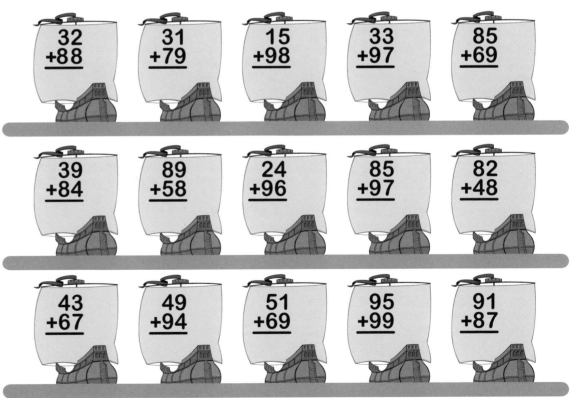

```
  32        31        15        33        85
+ 88      + 79      + 98      + 97      + 69
```

```
  39        89        24        85        82
+ 84      + 58      + 96      + 97      + 48
```

```
  43        49        51        95        91
+ 67      + 94      + 69      + 99      + 87
```

Try to complete each chart in less than 2 minutes.
The first one is solved for you.

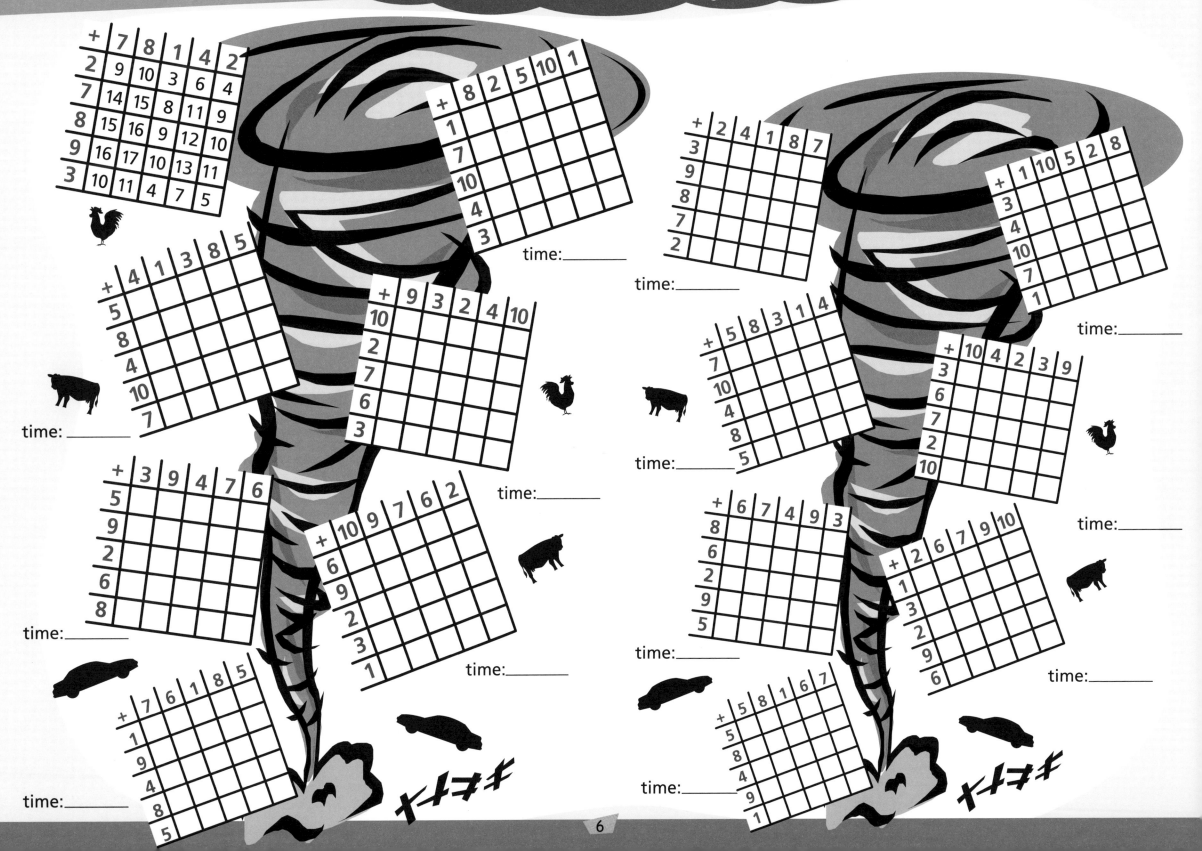

+	7	8	1	4	2
2	9	10	3	6	4
7	14	15	8	11	9
8	15	16	9	12	10
9	16	17	10	13	11
3	10	11	4	7	5

+	8	2	5	10	1
1					
7					
10					
4					
3					

time:_____

+	2	4	1	8	7
3					
9					
8					
7					
2					

time:_____

+	1	10	5	2	8
3					
4					
10					
7					
1					

time:_____

+	4	1	3	8	5
5					
8					
4					
10					
7					

time:_____

+	9	3	2	4	10
10					
2					
7					
6					
3					

time:_____

+	5	8	3	1	4
7					
10					
4					
8					
5					

time:_____

+	10	4	2	3	9
3					
6					
7					
2					
10					

time:_____

+	3	9	4	7	6
5					
9					
2					
6					
8					

time:_____

+	10	9	7	6	2
6					
9					
2					
3					
1					

time:_____

+	6	7	4	9	3
8					
6					
2					
9					
5					

time:_____

+	2	6	7	9	10
1					
3					
2					
9					
6					

time:_____

+	7	6	1	8	5
1					
9					
4					
8					
5					

time:_____

+	5	8	1	6	7
5					
8					
4					
9					
1					

time:_____

THE KEY TO THE CODE LETTERS

Use Addition to reveal the secret message!

Example

```
   0        5        4        3
 + 1      + 4      + 4      + 4
 ---      ---      ---      ---
   1        9        8        7
```

↓ ↓ ↓ ↓

S **O** **I** **L**

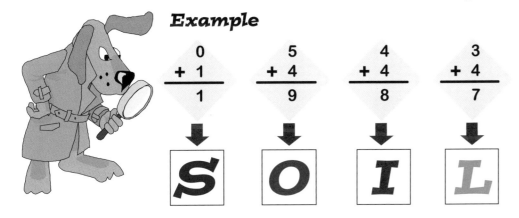

```
1 = S    4 = D    7 = L
2 = G    5 = V    8 = I
3 = W    6 = E    9 = O
```

Add.
Use the Key to match each sum with a code letter. Then fill in each letter of the message. **What's the secret message?**

```
   6        4        3        3        6        3        7        2        0
 + 2      + 3      + 6      + 2      + 0      + 1      + 2      + 0      + 1
 ---      ---      ---      ---      ---      ---      ---      ---      ---
```

↓

[ ] [ ] [ ] [ ] [ ] [ ] [ ] [ ] [ ]

ADDITION RIDDLES: MORE CODE TO CRACK!

```
1 = S    4 = D    7 = L
2 = G    5 = V    8 = I
3 = W    6 = E    9 = O
```

What did the burglar leave at the scene of the crime?

```
   2        4        6        3        4
 + 0      + 3      + 3      + 2      + 2
 ---      ---      ---      ---      ---
```

[ ] [ ] [ ] [ ] [ ]

```
1 = S    4 = D    7 = L
2 = G    5 = V    8 = I
3 = W    6 = E    9 = O
```

He also left a thread from his what?

```
   1        5        3        2        4        1
 + 0      + 2      + 3      + 4      + 1      + 5
 ---      ---      ---      ---      ---      ---
```

[ ] [ ] [ ] [ ] [ ] [ ]

Subtraction without regrouping

When we subtract, we find the **difference**. First we subtract the ones, then the tens, and then the hundreds.

Subtract the ones:	Now subtract the tens:	Now subtract the hundreds:
7 5 **9** − 2 4 **3** **6**	7 **5** 9 − 2 **4** 3 **1** 6	**7** 5 9 − **2** 4 3 **5** 1 6

Try these.

1 9 − 1 7	5 6 − 2 1	3 3 − 1 2
9 8 − 7 4	8 6 − 5 5	4 6 − 1 4

Subtraction with regrouping

When we subtract, sometimes we have to regroup. See how this works in this example.

4 **5**
 − 2 **7**

We start with the ones. Since we can't subtract 7 from 5, we need to regroup. We take 1 ten from the tens place and add it to the 5 ones so that we now have 15 ones and 3 tens.

³4 ¹5
 − 2 7
 8

Now we can subtract the ones column, 15-7=8.

Next, we subtract the tens column.

³4 5
 − 2 7
 1 8

Since we regrouped 1 ten away from the 4 tens, there are 3 tens left. We subtract 3-2=1. Now we have found the difference, 18.

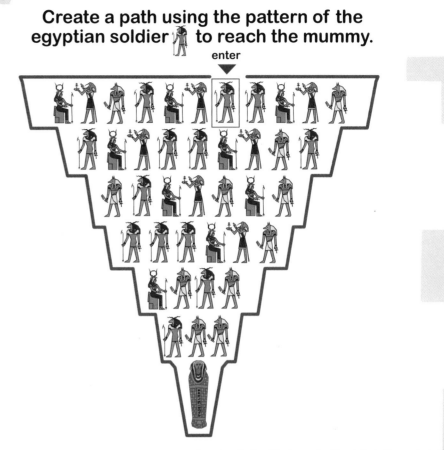

Create a path using the pattern of the egyptian soldier to reach the mummy.

enter

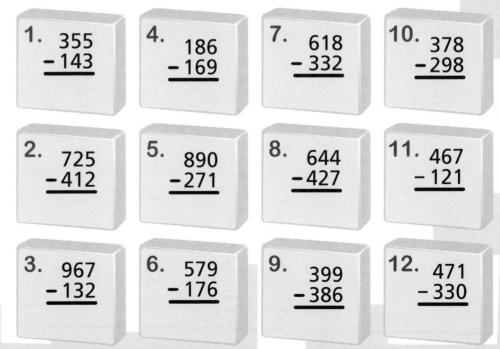

Practice subtraction. Fill in the missing numbers.

1. 355 − 143	4. 186 − 169	7. 618 − 332	10. 378 − 298
2. 725 − 412	5. 890 − 271	8. 644 − 427	11. 467 − 121
3. 967 − 132	6. 579 − 176	9. 399 − 386	12. 471 − 330

Fact Families: Addition and Subtraction

Every addition fact has a related subtraction fact. These are called fact families. Knowing one fact helps you know the other facts in the family. Look at this array as an example.

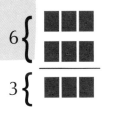

The fact family for this array is:

6 { ... }
3 { ... }

6+3=9
3+6=9
9-3=6
9-6=3

Use each array to complete the fact family beside it.

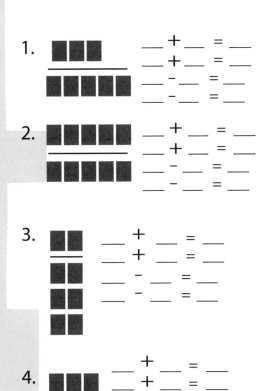

1. ___ + ___ = ___
    ___ + ___ = ___
    ___ - ___ = ___
    ___ - ___ = ___

2. ___ + ___ = ___
    ___ + ___ = ___
    ___ - ___ = ___
    ___ - ___ = ___

3. ___ + ___ = ___
    ___ + ___ = ___
    ___ - ___ = ___
    ___ - ___ = ___

4. ___ + ___ = ___
    ___ + ___ = ___
    ___ - ___ = ___
    ___ - ___ = ___

5. ___ + ___ = ___
    ___ + ___ = ___
    ___ - ___ = ___
    ___ - ___ = ___

6. ___ + ___ = ___
    ___ + ___ = ___
    ___ - ___ = ___
    ___ - ___ = ___

7. ___ + ___ = ___
    ___ + ___ = ___
    ___ - ___ = ___
    ___ - ___ = ___

8. ___ + ___ = ___
    ___ + ___ = ___
    ___ - ___ = ___
    ___ - ___ = ___

Subtraction practice.
Fill in the missing numbers.

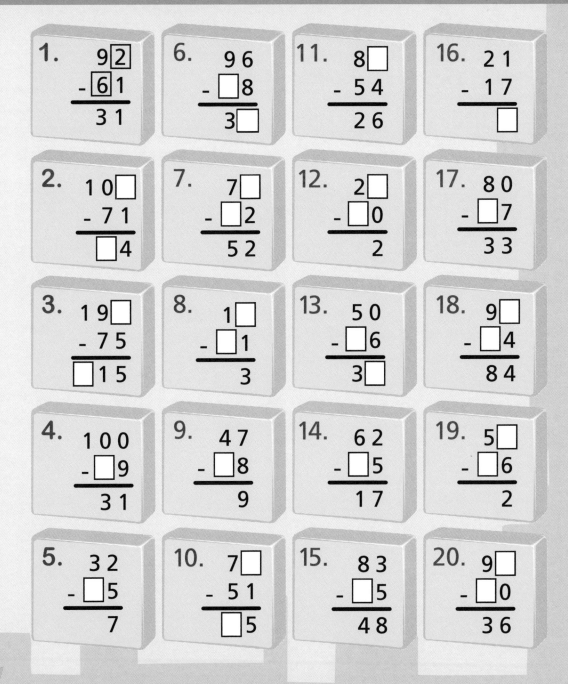

1. 9 [2]
    - [6] 1
    _____
    3 1

2. 1 0 ☐
    - 7 1
    _____
    ☐ 4

3. 1 9 ☐
    - 7 5
    _____
    ☐ 1 5

4. 1 0 0
    - ☐ 9
    _____
    3 1

5. 3 2
    - ☐ 5
    _____
    7

6. 9 6
    - ☐ 8
    _____
    3 ☐

7. 7 ☐
    - ☐ 2
    _____
    5 2

8. 1 ☐
    - ☐ 1
    _____
    3

9. 4 7
    - ☐ 8
    _____
    9

10. 7 ☐
    - 5 1
    _____
    ☐ 5

11. 8 ☐
    - 5 4
    _____
    2 6

12. 2 ☐
    - ☐ 0
    _____
    2

13. 5 0
    - ☐ 6
    _____
    3 ☐

14. 6 2
    - ☐ 5
    _____
    1 7

15. 8 3
    - ☐ 5
    _____
    4 8

16. 2 1
    - 1 7
    _____
    ☐

17. 8 0
    - ☐ 7
    _____
    3 3

18. 9 ☐
    - ☐ 4
    _____
    8 4

19. 5 ☐
    - ☐ 6
    _____
    2

20. 9 ☐
    - ☐ 0
    _____
    3 6

Multiplication

Multiplication is a way to add numbers faster. Multiplication is adding the same number together multiple times. When numbers are multiplied, the answer is called the **product**.

How many scoops of ice cream are there?

3 + 3 + 3 + 3 = 12
4 groups of 3 scoops = 12
4 x 3 = 12

__3__ + __3__ + __3__ + __3__ = __12__ scoops

Look at the pictures. Fill in the blanks.

___ groups of ___ crayons

= ___ x ___

= ____

___ groups of ___ pennies

= ___ x ___

= ____

___ groups of ___ peas in pod

= ___ x ___

= ____

___ groups of ___ beans

= ___ x ___

= ____

Complete the addition and multiplication sentences.

How many petals?

__ + __ + __ = ____

__ groups of 5 petals = ____

__ x __ = ____

There are ___ petals.

How many bees?

__ + __ + __ + __ + __ + __ = __

___ groups of 2 bees = ____

__ x __ = ____

There are ___ bees.

How many ladybugs?

__ + __ + __ + __ + __ = ____

__ groups of 4 ladybugs = ____

__ x __ = ____

There are ___ ladybugs.

How many butterflies?

__ + __ + __ + __ + __ + __ = ____

___ groups of 3 butterflies = ____

__ x __ = ____

There are ___ butterflies.

Write a multiplication sentence to match each group of beads.

__ X __ = __

__ X __ = __

__ X __ = __

__ X __ = __

Practice multiplication tables.

1 x 2 = ____	1 x 5 = ____	1 x 3 = ____	1 x 7 = ____
2 x 2 = ____	2 x 5 = ____	2 x 3 = ____	2 x 7 = ____
3 x 2 = ____	3 x 5 = ____	3 x 3 = ____	3 x 7 = ____
4 x 2 = ____	4 x 5 = ____	4 x 3 = ____	4 x 7 = ____
5 x 2 = ____	5 x 5 = ____	5 x 3 = ____	5 x 7 = ____
6 x 2 = ____	6 x 5 = ____	6 x 3 = ____	6 x 7 = ____
7 x 2 = ____	7 x 5 = ____	7 x 3 = ____	7 x 7 = ____

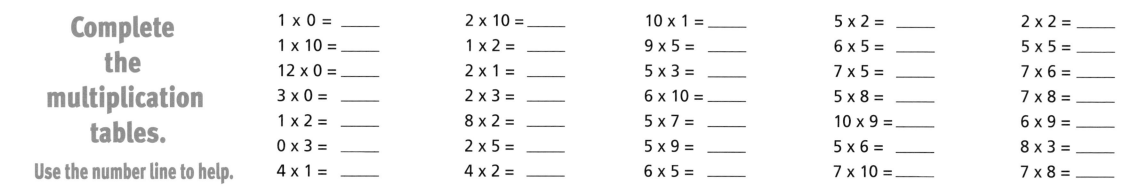

1 x 5   2 x 5

0 1 2 3 4 5 6 7 8 9 10 11 12 13 14 15 16 17 18 19 20 21 22 23 24 25 26 27 28 29 30 31 32 33 34 35 36 37 38 39 40 41 42 43 44 45 46 47 48 49 50

51 52 53 54 55 56 57 58 59 60 61 62 63 64 65 66 67 68 69 70 71 72 73 74 75 76 77 78 79 80 81 82 83 84 85 86 87 88 89 90 91 92 93 94 95 96 97 98 99 100

Complete the multiplication tables.

Use the number line to help.

1 x 0 = ____	2 x 10 = ____	10 x 1 = ____	5 x 2 = ____	2 x 2 = ____
1 x 10 = ____	1 x 2 = ____	9 x 5 = ____	6 x 5 = ____	5 x 5 = ____
12 x 0 = ____	2 x 1 = ____	5 x 3 = ____	7 x 5 = ____	7 x 6 = ____
3 x 0 = ____	2 x 3 = ____	6 x 10 = ____	5 x 8 = ____	7 x 8 = ____
1 x 2 = ____	8 x 2 = ____	5 x 7 = ____	10 x 9 = ____	6 x 9 = ____
0 x 3 = ____	2 x 5 = ____	5 x 9 = ____	5 x 6 = ____	8 x 3 = ____
4 x 1 = ____	4 x 2 = ____	6 x 5 = ____	7 x 10 = ____	7 x 8 = ____

Complete the multiplication box. Some are done for you.

X	1	2	3	4	5	6	7	8	9	10	11	12
1	1											
2		4										
3			9									
4				16								
5					25							
6						36						
7							49					
8								64				
9									81			
10										100		
11											121	
12												144

Multiply through the mountain and down the river.

Start

3 x 9 =

7 x 4 =

2 x 8 =

9 x 5 =

8 x 7 =

4 x 2 =

7 x 7 =

8 x 6 =

9 x 3 =

8 x 5 =

8 x 8 =

6 x 9 =

9 x 8 =

5 x 5 =

8 x 3 =

2 x 10 =

6 x 6 =

1 x 4 =

6 x 5 =

4 x 10 =

7 x 5 =

10 x 8 =

5 x 8 =

11

Finish ●

Division is equal sharing or groupings.

The answer to your division question is called a **quotient**.

In multiplication the answer is called the **product**.

Can you remember what the answers for adding and subtracting are called?

Adding _____ **Subtracting** _____

This shows 40 baseballs.

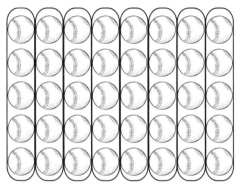

Divide the baseballs into groups of 5.
How many groups are there? ___8___
This shows $40 \div 8 =$ ___5___
This is part of a multiplication and
division fact family: $5 \times 8 = 40$
$8 \times 5 = 40$
$40 \div 5 = 8$
$40 \div 8 = 5$

Try the following questions on your own!

1. Circle in groups of 3.

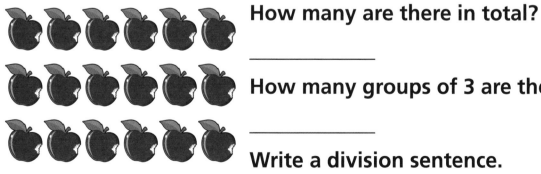

How many are there in total?

_____

How many groups of 3 are there?

_____

Write a division sentence.

_____

Write a multiplication fact using the same numbers.

_____

2. Circle in groups of 4.

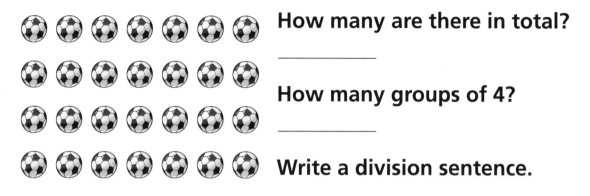

How many are there in total?

_____

How many groups of 4?

_____

Write a division sentence.

_____

Write a multiplication fact using the same numbers.

_____

3. Circle in groups of 2.

How many are there in total?

_____

How many groups of 2?

_____

Write a division sentence.

_____

Write a multiplication fact using the same numbers.

Write a division sentence to match each group.

4. 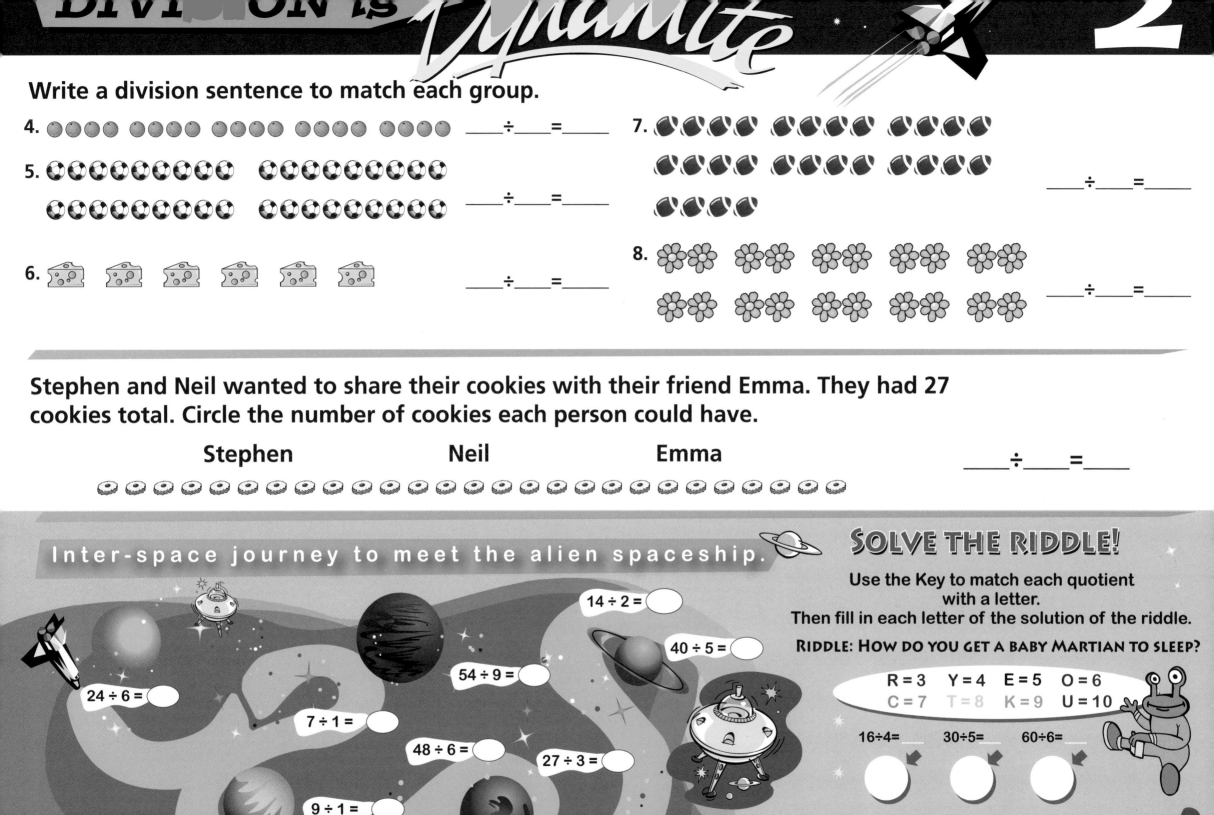 _____ ÷ _____ = _____

5. _____ ÷ _____ = _____

6. _____ ÷ _____ = _____

7. _____ ÷ _____ = _____

8. _____ ÷ _____ = _____

Stephen and Neil wanted to share their cookies with their friend Emma. They had 27 cookies total. Circle the number of cookies each person could have.

Stephen   Neil   Emma

_____ ÷ _____ = _____

Inter-space journey to meet the alien spaceship.

14 ÷ 2 = ◯

40 ÷ 5 = ◯

54 ÷ 9 = ◯

24 ÷ 6 = ◯

7 ÷ 1 = ◯

48 ÷ 6 = ◯

27 ÷ 3 = ◯

9 ÷ 1 = ◯

42 ÷ 6 = ◯

24 ÷ 3 = ◯

SOLVE THE RIDDLE!

Use the Key to match each quotient with a letter.
Then fill in each letter of the solution of the riddle.

RIDDLE: HOW DO YOU GET A BABY MARTIAN TO SLEEP?

R = 3   Y = 4   E = 5   O = 6
C = 7   T = 8   K = 9   U = 10

16÷4=____   30÷5=____   60÷6=____

◯   ◯   ◯

21÷7=____   18÷3=____   35÷5=____   90÷10=____   40÷8=____   64÷8=____

◯   ◯   ◯   ◯   ◯   ◯

13

Pictograph

A **pictograph** is a graph that uses pictures or symbols to show data.

Read the graph and answer the following questions.

20 students in Ms. Bertin's class did a survey to find out what their favourite type of healthy snack was. This graph shows their data.

Favourite Snacks in Ms. Bertin's Class	
Fruit	🍎 🍎 🍎 🍎
Granola	🍪 🍪 🍪
Vegetables	🥕
Cheese and Crackers	🧀 🧀

1. If there are 20 students in Ms. Bertin's class, how many students does each piece of food represent? _____

2. What was the most popular snack? _____

3. What was the least popular snack? _____

4. How many people liked fruit best? _____

5. How many people liked granola best? _____

6. How many people liked vegetables best? _____

7. How many people liked cheese and crackers best? _____

8. What is your favourite type of healthy snack? _____

Bar graph

The graph below is called a **bar graph**.

Read the graph and answer the following questions.

This bar graph tells how much of each type of fruit Grampa Jim grows on his farm.

Each block stands for 10 baskets of fruit.

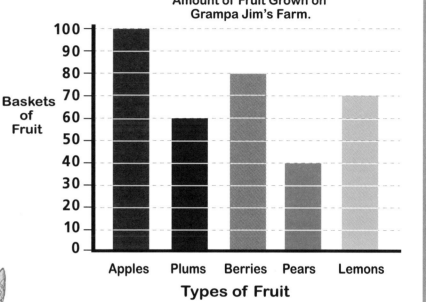

Amount of Fruit Grown on Grampa Jim's Farm.

1. What does the graph tell us about? _____

2. How many baskets of apples does Grampa Jim grow? _____

3. How many more berries than pears does he grow? _____

4. What does Grampa Jim grow the most of? _____

5. What does Grampa Jim grow the least of? _____

6. How many types of fruit does Grampa Jim grow? _____

7. How much fruit does Grampa Jim grow all together? _____

Time

Write the time shown.

4 : 00

_____ : _____   _____ : _____   _____ : _____

_____ : _____   _____ : _____   _____ : _____   _____ : _____

_____ : _____   _____ : _____   _____ : _____   _____ : _____

_____ minutes after _____   _____ minutes before _____   _____ minutes before _____   _____ minutes after _____
_____ minutes after _____

Draw the hands to match the time on the digital clock.

| 9:05 | 12:50 | 2:10 | 5:35 |

15

Time Maze

Start

8 : 20

7 : 55

6 : 10

9 : 15

3 : 00

9 : 30

8 : 00

1 : 40

4 : 05

5 : 55

4 : 00

9 : 20

11 : 30

3 : 40

9 : 00

5 : 05

3 : 50

End

Fractions tell about equal parts of a whole or set.

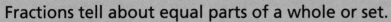

$\dfrac{2}{5}$ **Numerator**
Denominator

There are 5 parts to this whole. 2 parts are shaded.

The **denominator** is the bottom number in a fraction. It tells how many parts there are in total in the whole or set. In this case the denominator is 5. The **numerator** is the top number in a fraction. It is the number of equal parts being identified. In this case the numerator is 2.

The line separating the numerator and denominator means 'out of'. This fraction is $\frac{2}{5}$. It means 2 equal parts 'out of' 5 total parts.

Pizza Parts

Look at the pizza.
Some slices have pepperoni,
some have mushrooms,
some have olives,
and some are plain.

Answer the questions
about the parts
of the pizza.
Some are answered for you.

1. How many slices of pizza are there in total? __10__

2. What fraction of the pizza is plain? __$\dfrac{3}{10}$__

3. What fraction has pepperoni? _____

4. What fraction has olives? _____

5. What fraction has mushrooms? _____

Write a fraction that identifies the coloured part of each shape.

   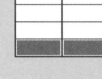 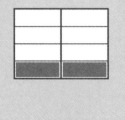

$\dfrac{1}{2}$ ____ ____ ____

 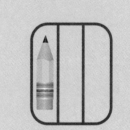 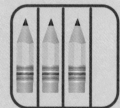

____ ____ ____ ____

____ ____ ____ ____

____ ____ ____ ____

$2.00 $1.00   25¢   10¢   5¢   1¢ $5.00 $10.00 $20.00

$1.45 $0.89 $3.67 $7.92 $2.37 $0.25 $1.18 $4.50 $21.95

1. How much would it cost to buy the marbles and the doll?

2. What is the difference in cost between the basketball and the bouncy ball?

3. How much would the boomerang, the dinosaur and the lollipop cost all together?

4. If Matthew has $9.00 does he have enough money to buy the teddy bear and the toy truck?

If so, how much change would he get?

5. If you had $15.00, how many items could you buy from the store?
List them and the total amount they would cost.
Answers will vary.

Write a friendly letter.

A letter is a written message that we can send to a friend, relative or even somone we don't know, like an author. Friendly letters include information about yourself and ask questions about how your friend or relative is doing.

123 Fanway St.
Smallville, ON
A1B 2C4
July 12, 2009

Dear Sam,
How is camp? Mom, Dad and I miss you. What is the food like there? I can't wait until I'm old enough to go to camp! Write back soon.

Love,
Mike

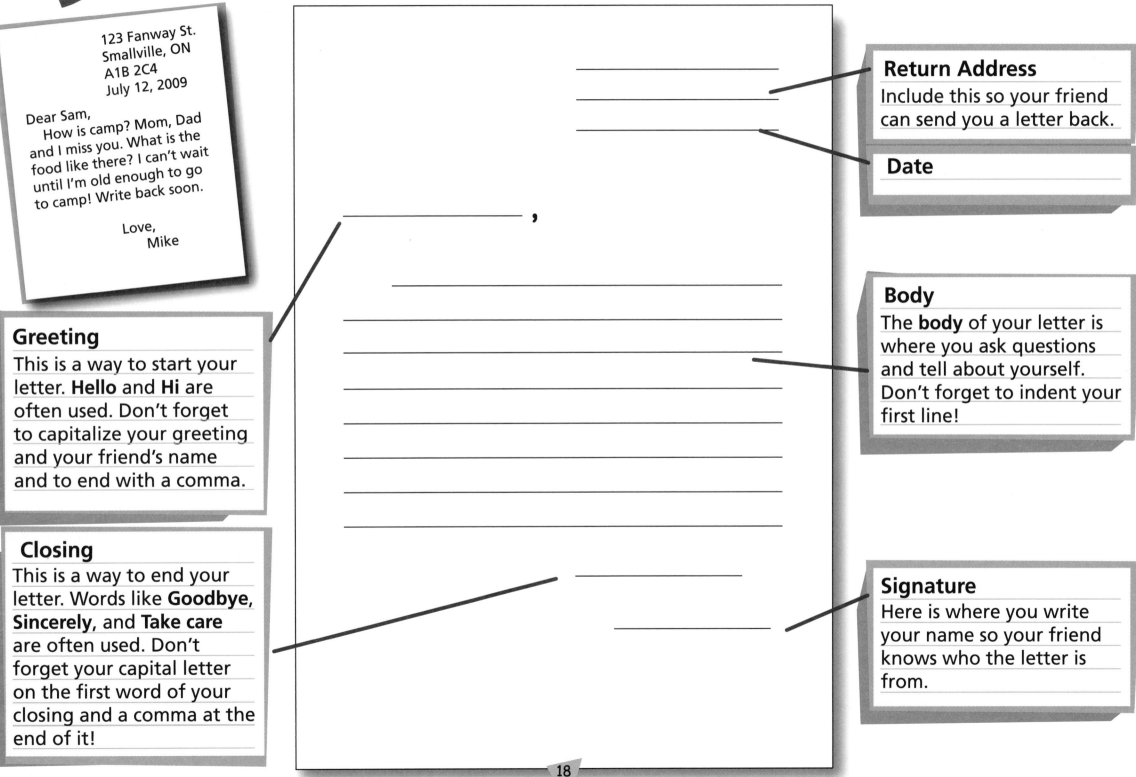

_____ ,

Return Address
Include this so your friend can send you a letter back.

Date

Greeting
This is a way to start your letter. **Hello** and **Hi** are often used. Don't forget to capitalize your greeting and your friend's name and to end with a comma.

Body
The **body** of your letter is where you ask questions and tell about yourself. Don't forget to indent your first line!

Closing
This is a way to end your letter. Words like **Goodbye**, **Sincerely**, and **Take care** are often used. Don't forget your capital letter on the first word of your closing and a comma at the end of it!

Signature
Here is where you write your name so your friend knows who the letter is from.

Picture Dictionary

A picture dictionary is used to help understand the meaning of words and to find out how they are spelled. It is especially useful for defining nouns.

A noun is a person, place, or thing.

Look at the examples below. Think of another word for each letter. Draw a picture and write the word.

Aa	Bb	Cc	Dd	Ee	Ff	Gg	Hh	Ii
ambulance	butterfly	calculator	dragon	elephant	fingerprint	giraffe	helicopter	insect

Jj	Kk	Ll	Mm	Nn	Oo	Pp	Qq	Rr
juggling	knapsack	leaf	microscope	notebook	octopus	parachute	queen	rhinoceros

Picture Dictionary

A picture dictionary is used to help understand the meaning of words and to find out how they are spelled. It is especially useful for defining nouns.

Look at the examples below. Think of another word for each letter. Draw a picture and write the word.

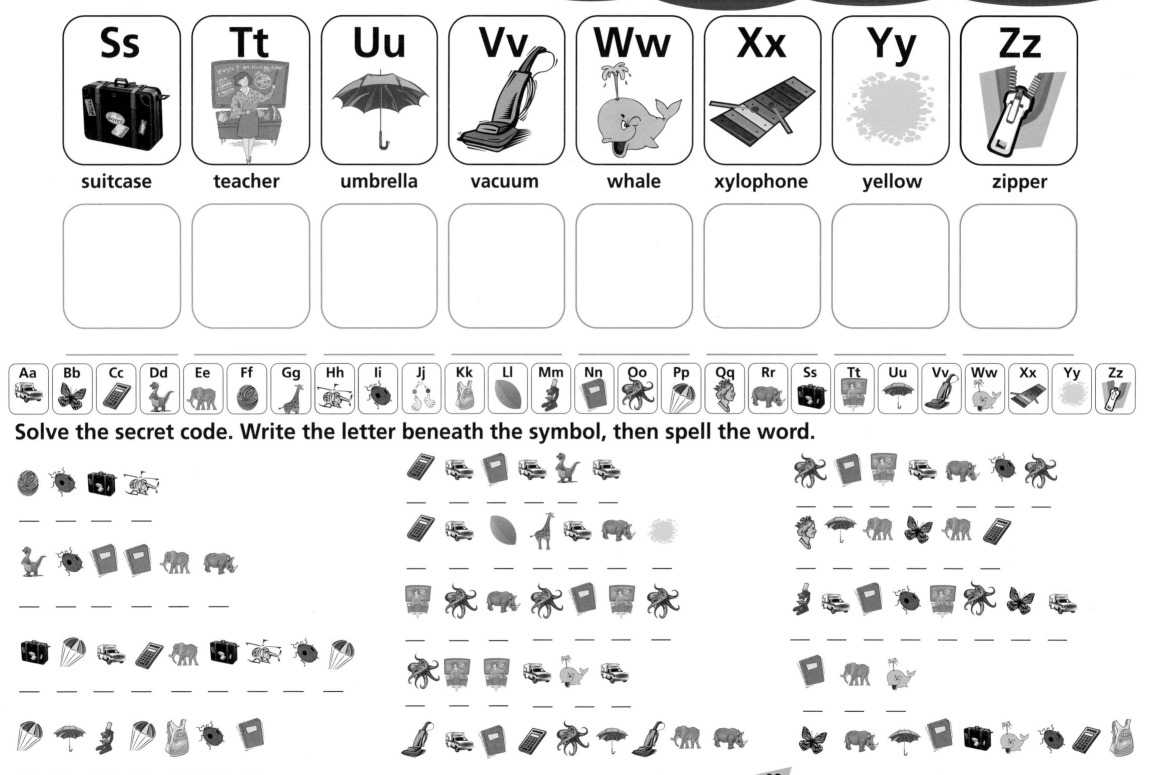

Ss	Tt	Uu	Vv	Ww	Xx	Yy	Zz
suitcase	teacher	umbrella	vacuum	whale	xylophone	yellow	zipper

Solve the secret code. Write the letter beneath the symbol, then spell the word.

20

Design a Poster

Design your own poster advertising your favourite book.
Remember to include why someone would want to read this book.
Draw a picture that will attract a reader's attention!

Below is a poster advertising a book.

Draw your poster here.

Draft outline for your favourite book.

Title of book	
Why it's good	
Picture ideas	

Statements and Questions

Statements are sentences that tell information. They always start with a capital and end in a period.

Question sentences are asking for information. They always start with capital and end with a question mark (?). Many of them begin with asking words like *Who, Do, Did, How, What, Where, Why*.

Complete the final punctuation.

1. How old are you ____
2. I like to eat chocolate ice cream ____
3. My favourite food is pizza ____
4. What did you do on your vacation ____
5. How fast did you run ____
6. My dog can play catch with me ____
7. I got an A on my last math test ____
8. Does your teacher give you homework ____
9. The weather today is sunny and bright ____
10. I want to have a fish for a pet ____
11. Who is your best friend ____
12. My friend Mei Lei and I like to play soccer ____

Imagine you went to a birthday party. Make up 2 of your own statement sentences about the party.

1. _____
2. _____

Make up 2 questions your mother or father might ask you about the party.

1. _____
2. _____

Nouns

A **common noun** is a person, place or thing.

Read the following passage and underline the nouns.

Yesterday I went to the store with my friend Rashida. We both wanted to buy some candy. We counted all of our coins and decided to buy some candy fish, a chocolate bar and a bag of chips. Rashida and I decided to share our treats while she walked her dog. She told me her dog's name was Shadow.

Place each noun you have underlined in the box it matches.

Person	Place	Thing

Proper Nouns

Proper nouns are nouns that name a specific person, place or thing. Proper nouns always start with capital letters.
Example:
common noun – boy, city, holiday
proper nouns – Omed, Ottawa, Christmas

Put the following nouns in the correct box. Be sure to capitalize the proper nouns.

thanksgiving
uncle
student
niagara falls
children
girl
barbara
school
c.n. tower
pencil

china
brother
sister
tuesday
ontario
city
ms. bertin
florida
cook
dr. landry

book
july
parent
library
monday
calgary
camp
parking lot
dog

Common Nouns

Proper Nouns

An **adjective** describes (or modifies) a **noun**. Adjectives tell us what nouns are like — how they look, sound, feel, smell, or taste, and how many there are (or how much), what kind they are, and so on.

Example:
The **shiny** spaceship, filled with **awesome** astronauts, landed on the **magnificent** moon.

Shiny modifies *spaceship*.
Awesome modifies *astronauts*.
Magnificent modifies *moon*.

Shiny, **awesome**, and **magnificent** are adjectives.

Silly Stories

Use adjectives from the list below or think up your own to finish these stories. Be as silly as you like. Then read your stories out loud.

A Lunchtime Surprise

One _____ day I had the most _____ lunch of my life. When I opened my lunch bag, here's what I found: the _____ cheese smelled like _____ socks; the bread was _____; the _____ apple had _____ spots on it; and my milk had turned _____! That was the most _____ meal I've ever eaten.

The Costume Shop

In our town, we have no ordinary costume shop. Some people say it's _____ or even downright _____! There are _____ wizard robes covered with _____ sparkles. The _____ gorilla suits feel as _____ as a(n) _____ sweater. The _____ princess gowns are so _____ that you might need to wear _____ sunglasses to look at them. There are _____ wigs, _____ shoes, _____ wands, _____ hats, and other many other _____ things. You should stop by there next Halloween.

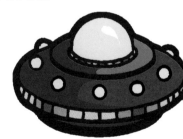

The Aliens

One _____ morning I woke up, looked out my window, and saw aliens in our backyard. After their _____ spaceship landed, I watched three _____ aliens climb out and look around. The first alien had _____ hair, _____ eyes, and _____ fingers. The second alien had _____ ears and a _____ nose that was covered in _____ bumps. The third alien had _____ arms and _____ legs and the _____-est tail I have ever seen. After that day, I stopped eating so many _____ snacks before bed.

Some Amazing, Adventurous Adjectives

slippery	tricky	fuzzy	delicious	teeny	billions	bumpy	salty
shiny	blue	gurgling	big	tiny	some	careful	lucky
shaky	yellow	chilly	bigger	teensy-	several	heroic	
boiled	polka-dot	noisy	biggest	weensy	many	exciting	
amazing	striped	sticky	huge	one	clanging	memorable	
rotten	stinky	brave	enormous	five	sparkly	invisible	

23

Verbs

Remember: **Verbs** are **action words** like *shout*, *run*, *think*, *shine*, *hop*, *lick*, and also **being words** (called linking verbs) like *am*, *is*, *are*. There are also **helping verbs** that **help the main verb** tell about the action like *can* wink, *may* leave, *must* ask. All sentences need verbs.

Tickle the baby on the foot.
(doing verb)

The sweater **is** fuzzy.
(being verb)

When you **are** lost, you **must yell** for help.
(being verb + helping verb + action verb)

Match the Present Tense.

I _____ cookies.

wish

loves

play

I _____ for a warm day.

My dog _____ me.

I _____ in the backyard.

bake

Past Tense

We often use verbs in the past tense. They tell us what happened in the past.

*This morning I **got** dressed, **ate** breakfast, **brushed** my teeth, and then **rode** my bike to the park.*

*In olden times, people **travelled** by horse and buggy.*

*After our long hike this morning, we **were** tired.*

Past Tense Crossword Puzzle

Complete the puzzle with the past tense of each verb. The first one is done for you.

Across:
1. talk ___talked___
2. see _____
3. open _____
4. are _____

Down:
5. eat _____
6. listen _____
7. write _____
8. do _____

24

Tired Verbs and Vivid Verbs

Some verbs, like *said* and *went*, get used a lot. They can make a sentence sound tired. You can wake up tired sentences by using more vivid verbs.

Tired Verb: said

Vivid Verbs:	Think of other vivid verbs:
whispered	_____
croaked	_____
giggled	_____
moaned	_____
cheered	_____
hissed	_____
bellowed	_____

Write a vivid verb in sentence below. Use the list or think of your own.

"It's time to come home!" _____ the mother.

"We won," _____ the hockey player.

"Your costume is funny," _____ the boy.

The singer _____ , "My throat hurts."

"I am finished my homework," _____ Anna.

"Shhh," _____ the librarian.

Tired Verb: went

Vivid Verbs:	Think of other vivid verbs:
skipped	_____
shuffled	_____
raced	_____
strode	_____
marched	_____
scampered	_____
hopped	_____
limped	_____

Write a vivid verb in sentence below. Use the list or think of your own.

We _____ all the way around the track.

The children _____ to the park.

The monkeys _____ up the tree.

The tired runner _____ home to rest.

A mouse _____ across the floor.

Adverbs

How? When? Where? How much?

Adverbs always tell more about (or modify) verbs, adjectives, and even other adverbs. They always tell us *how, when, where,* or *how much.* Many adverbs end in ly.

How
I carefully walked around the broken glass.
How did I walk? **Carefully.**
The duck swam lazily across the pond.
How did the duck swim? **Lazily.**

When
He promptly returned the library book.
When did he return the library book?
Promptly.
My brother practices the piano daily.
When does he practice? **Daily.**

Where
Wait here while I get my coat.
Wait where? **Here.**
Water sprayed everywhere when the wet dog shook himself.
Sprayed where? **Everywhere.**

How much
I am so happy with my new puppy.
How happy am I? **So** happy.
You are very tall.
How tall? **Very** tall.

How?
When?
Where?
How much?

Adverb Word Search

Find each of the adverbs!

How adverbs

skillfully
sloppily
carefully
quickly
slowly
gently
roughly
crossly

When adverbs

never
always
yesterday
now
often
today
last
rarely

Where adverbs

here
there
away

How much adverbs

so
very
extremely
nearly
completely
totally
partially

g	e	n	t	l	y	b	x	t	s	o
s	r	b	t	h	n	n	s	h	k	a
l	o	a	f	l	e	k	l	e	i	p
o	u	o	c	n	v	a	o	r	l	a
w	g	f	a	e	e	l	p	e	l	r
l	h	t	r	a	r	w	p	o	f	t
y	l	e	e	r	h	a	i	u	u	i
t	y	n	f	l	c	y	l	d	l	a
n	o	w	u	y	f	s	y	l	l	l
l	a	f	l	h	e	r	e	y	y	l
a	w	r	l	c	r	o	s	s	l	y
s	a	o	y	q	u	i	c	k	l	y
t	y	i	r	s	t	t	o	d	a	y
y	e	s	t	e	r	d	a	y	g	u
b	r	a	r	e	l	y	y	r	g	f
e	x	t	r	e	m	e	l	y	v	t
l	c	o	m	p	l	e	t	e	l	y
t	o	t	a	l	l	y	v	e	r	y

Homonyms and Homophones

Homophones and **homonyms** are both words that sound the same but have different meanings. **Homophones** are also spelled differently. **See** (with your eyes) and **sea** (the ocean) are examples of homophones.

Homonyms have the same spelling. **Bear** (the animal) and **bear** (to carry a heavy load) are examples of homonyms.

Homonyms

Draw lines to the different meanings of each word:

tap	a big furry animal
	hit gently
work	winter, spring, summer and fall
	a job
hit	what a baseball player likes to steal
	carry
base	sad
	the colour of the sky
bear	a very popular song
	water comes out of it
season	a piece of art
	strike forcefully
blue	the bottom part of something
	add spices

Homophones

Pick the right word each picture. Write it in the box.

eight   ate   choose   chews   piece   peace

dear   deer   pair   pear   heard   herd   tale   tail

scent sent cent   they're there their   bear   bare

hear   here   aunt   ant   too   to   two

26

Urban communities are areas where many people live, like big cities.
You can use a map to find out lots of information about urban communities.

Parts of a Map

A COMPASS ROSE shows direction.

The **SCALE** tells about distance.

The **LEGEND** uses symbols to represent different places that can be found on the map.

The **GRID** helps to find something specific by narrowing down where to look on the map.

Each square in the grid is called a **QUADRANT** and is identified by a letter and number (e.g. the hospital is at F5).

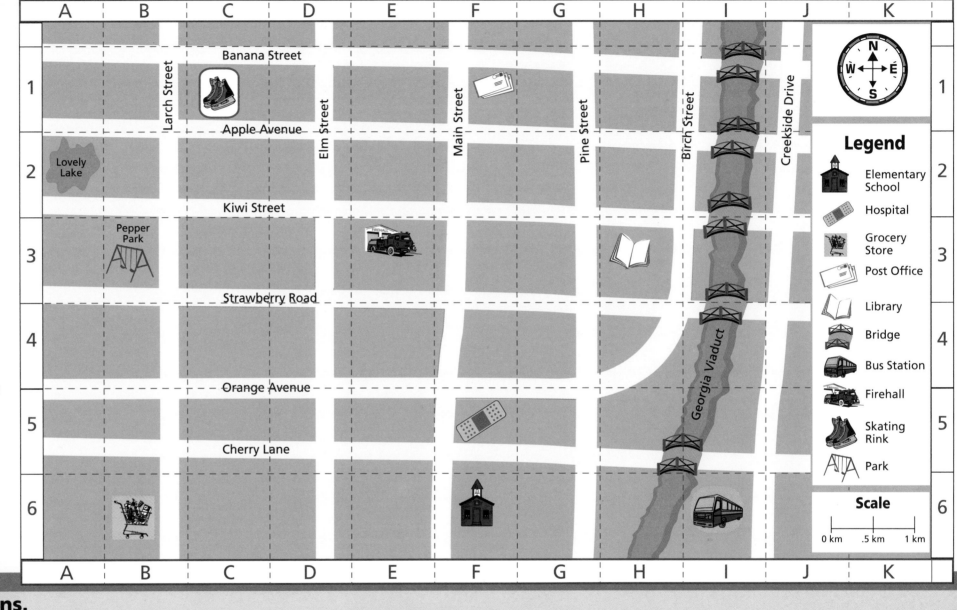

Legend

- Elementary School
- Hospital
- Grocery Store
- Post Office
- Library
- Bridge
- Bus Station
- Firehall
- Skating Rink
- Park

Scale

0 km   .5 km   1 km

Answer the questions.

In what quadrant can you find the library? _____

The school is at the corner of what streets? _____

How could you travel from the grocery store to the post office? _____

_____

What street is east of Main St.? _____

What is north of the grocery store? _____

What is west of the library? _____

In what quadrant is the firehall? _____

How could you travel from the park to the hospital? _____

_____

What street is east of the creek? _____

27

Some of them rhyme and some don't.
Below are three different types of poems.
Try your own!

Shape Poem

I love to
eat them in the summer
I love to eat them in the fall
Red, green, sweet, small
I love to eat them
anytime
at all!

A **shape poem** describes something while also looking like that image. Draw your shape then write your poem inside.

Acrostic Poem

H appy times

O n the ice

C hanging rooms are noisy

K eeping up with Coach

E arly morning practices

Y es! A goal!

An **acrostic poem** describes a noun. Try your name.

Haiku

Winter time is fun

Playing in the snow and ice

I love the outdoors

A **haiku** is a Japanese poem that follows a specific pattern. It is often about nature. It has 3 lines. The first has 5 syllables, the 2nd line has 7 syllables, and the 3rd line has 5 syllables.

Fables

Read the fable called The Lion and the Mouse:

One day a small mouse ran over the foot of a big lion. The lion grabbed the mouse and the mouse shouted, "Please let me go, lion! If you let me go, I will help you in return one day." The lion replied, "How could a small mouse like you ever help a brave lion like me?" The lion thought this idea was so funny that he started to laugh. He laughed so hard he let go of the mouse. "Who cares about a small mouse anyway," said the lion to himself. The following week the mouse was scurrying through the woods when he came across the lion, trapped in a hunter's ropes. The mouse thought, "I promised to help the lion, so I will." He began to chew the rope. He kept chewing until the ropes broke and lion was freed. "Thank you! Thank you!" exclaimed the lion. "I was wrong to have teased you for being too small." The moral of the story: Even small friends can do big things.

Now write your own fable. Use the following outline to help you build your ideas.

Main characters: (Think about characteristics of animals. If your main character is sly you might choose a fox. If it is wise you might choose an owl.)

- -

- -

Setting: (Where does your story take place? Is there more than one setting?)

- -

- -

Plot:

Beginning: (What happens in the beginning? Characters are introduced.)

- -

- -

- -

Middle: (What problem arises?)

- -

- -

- -

End: (How is the problem solved? What lesson is taught in this fable?)

- -

- -

- -

Now that you have planned out your own fable write it out.

- -

- -

- -

- -

- -

- -

- -

Blingpops on the Planet Droog

Writing Descriptions

Your spaceship has just touched down on the planet Droog, home of the mysterious creatures called blingpops. It is your job to send a report back to earth about the bling-pops. Luckily, you see a group of blingpops near your spaceship. Answer the questions using describing words to tell what they are like.

What does a blingpop's head look like?

What are its eyes, ears, nose, and mouth like?

What does a blingpop's body look like? What colour is it? How big is it? What shape is it?

How does a blingpop move around?

How do blingpops communicate?

Use your imagination to write a para-graph that tells more about what the blingpops look like and what they do. Make sure to include a topic sentence and to use describing words.

Draw a blingpop house here.

Draw what a blingpop looks like.

30

Writing Instructions

Instructions help you learn how to make or do something. For example, recipes, directions for taking tests, fire escape plans, or how-to manuals for video games all tell about how something is done.

Read the recipe below and answer the questions.

How to make cookies:

1. Find and gather the following ingredients.
   - 2 Mixing bowls
   - Measuring cups and spoons
   - Cookie sheet and cooling rack
   - 250 g all-purpose flour
   - 2 g baking soda
   - 3 g salt
   - 170 g unsalted butter, melted
   - 220 g packed brown sugar
   - 100 g white sugar
   - 15 ml vanilla extract
   - 1 egg
   - 335 g semisweet chocolate chips
2. Preheat the oven to 325° F (165° C). Grease cookie sheets or line with parchment paper.
3. Sift together the flour, baking soda, and salt; set aside.
4. In a medium bowl, cream together the melted butter, brown sugar, and white sugar until well blended. Beat in the vanilla and egg until light and creamy. Mix in the sifted ingredients until just blended. Stir in the chocolate chips using a wooden spoon. Drop cookie dough 60 g at a time onto the prepared cookie sheets. Cookies should be about 3 inches apart.
5. Bake for 15 to 17 minutes in the preheated oven, or until the edges are lightly toasted. Cool on baking sheets for a few minutes before transferring to wire racks to cool completely.

Questions:

1. How many ingredients on the list are food items? _____

2. How many ingredients do you mix together in the 3rd step? _____

3. What do you think is the hardest part about these instructions? _____
_____

Multiple choice questions:
Circle the correct answers.

4. This recipe tells about
a) why baking is important
b) how to make cookies
c) how to make chocolate cake
d) why eggs are healthy

Multiple choice questions continued:

5. The largest (according to number of grams) ingredient in this recipe is:
a. Sugar
b. Flour
c. Eggs
d. Chocolate chips

6. Which instructions are in the right order:
a. mix the flour, eggs, sugar, get bowls, blend well
b. turn on oven, gather ingredients, mix ingredients, let cool.
c. turn on oven, gather ingredients, mix ingredients, bake, let cool.
d. gather ingredients, turn on oven, mix ingredients, bake, let cool.

Write some instructions of your own!

Write instructions about how to make your favourite sandwich. Make sure you include any ingredients and the most important steps to take.

How to make a sandwich

_____
_____
_____
_____
_____
_____
_____
_____
_____
_____
_____
_____

Make sure you show your parent when you are finished!

Fact, Fiction and Opinion

Facts are something that are always true.
For example, 'Ottawa is the capital of Canada' is a fact.

Fiction is something that is made up. It is usually a story.
For example, 'pigs can fly' is fiction.

Opinion is what you think or feel about something. It's hard for someone to say if you are right or wrong. For example, 'Apples are delicious' is an opinion.

Write 'fact', 'fiction', or 'opinion' beside each sentence:

a. I make my own breakfast every morning._____

b. Oatmeal cookies are the best dessert._____

c. The province of Alberta is part of Canada._____

d. Pigs can build houses out of bricks. _____

e. Hamburgers are my favourite food. _____

f. People can buy groceries at the store. _____

g. There are 7 continents in the world. _____

h. My friend Sandeep is handsome. _____

i. A blue jay is a type of bird. _____

j. Falling snow is green. _____

k. A fish is a great pet to have. _____

l. Every child should play soccer. _____

Now think of some facts, opinions and fiction and write them on each line below.

Fact:_____

Fiction:_____

Opinion:_____

Fact:_____

Fiction:_____

Opinion:_____

Fact:_____

Fiction:_____

Opinion:_____

Now read the story and answer the questions.

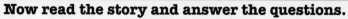

Many people love skiing. It is a winter sport that can be a great way to exercise. There are two main ways that people ski, downhill skiing and cross country skiing.

Downhill skis are attached to your feet at the front and back. You have to take a lift up to the top of the hill. It can be scary being so high up but coming down is terrific fun! You can twist, turn, jump, and even flip if you are really good. People who live near some mountains can ski all year, even in the summer, because there is snow at the top of the mountain.

Cross country skiing is a fun way to exercise in the winter anywhere there is snow! You can also cross country ski into wooded areas where you might see animals. Cross country skis are only attached to your toes so your heels can lift up. Sometimes on very snowy days you can even see people cross country skiing down the roads in a busy city. If you live in a place where there is snow you should try skiing. Whether it's downhill or cross country you're sure to have a great time!

True or False:

1. This story has both fiction and fact sentences. _____
2. You can downhill ski anywhere. _____
3. Skiing is a great way to exercise. _____
4. You can twist, turn and jump cross country skiing. _____
5. Many people think skiing is fun. _____

Multiple choice: Circle the correct answers.

1. Downhill skis attach to:
a) just your toes.
b) just your heels.
c) your toes and heels.
d) your elbow.

2. Skiing can sometimes be:
a) fun.
b) exciting.
c) scary.
d) all of the above.

3. You should try skiing if:
a) you live in a place where there is snow in winter.
b) you hate snow.
c) you live in a place where it is always warm.
d) you live on a boat.

4. People who live near mountains can:
a) try waterskiing.
b) can ski all year.
c) hike.
d) hate the snow.

5. Sometimes on very snowy days in the city you can see people:
a) sun tanning.
b) playing football.
c) skiing.
d) wearing shorts.

a b c d e f g h i j k l m n o p q r s t u v w x y z

A B C D E F G H I J K L M N O P Q R S T U V W X Y Z

Practice each group of letters.

1. ✏ *a, d, g, c, q*

a a a a

d d d d

g g g g

c c c c

q q q q

add

dad

2. ✏ *i, u, w, t*

i i i i

u u u u

w w w w

t t t t

it

wig

3. ✏ *e, l, h, f, j, b*

e e e e

l l l l

h h h h

f f f f

j j j j

b b b b

fell

life

4. ✏ *n, m, v, x*

n n n n

m m m m

v v v v

x x x x

watch

a b c d e f g h i j k l m n o p q r s t u v w x y z

A B C D E F G H I J K L M N O P Q R S T U V W X Y Z

Practice each group of letters.

5. ✏ p, r, s, o, y, z, k

p p p

r r r

s s s

o o o

y y y

z z z

k k k

zipper

yellow

7. ✏ **Now try your name.**

6. ✏ **Capital letters**

A A
B B
C C
D D
E E
F F
G G
H H
I I
J J
K K
L L
M M

N N
O O
P P
Q Q
R R
S S
T T
U U
V V
W W
X X
Y Y
Z Z

Answers

Play with Place Value - Page 2

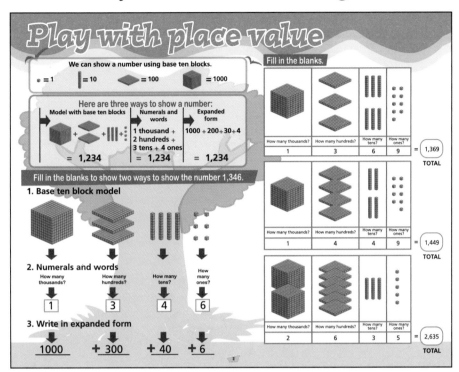

Skip Counting - Page 4

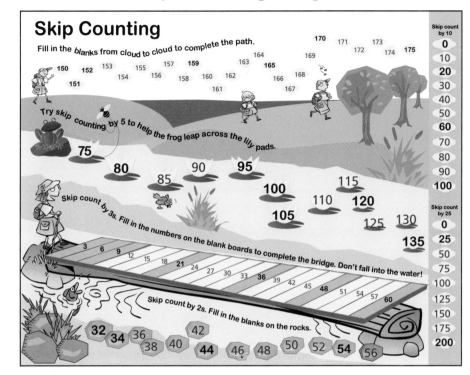

Place Value - Page 3

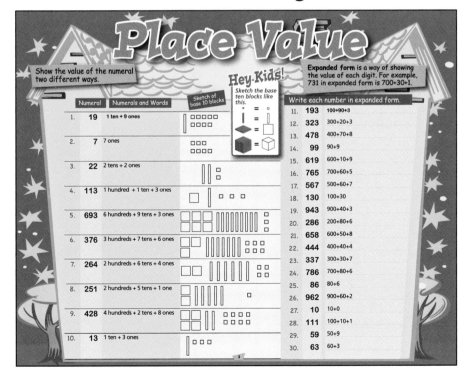

Addition 1 - Page 5

ADDITION + 1

Addition without regrouping

When we add, we find the **sum**. First we add the ones, then the tens, and then the hundreds.

25	26	156	816
+36	+48	+27	+159
61	74	183	975

Add the ones: Next add the tens: Next add the hundreds:

78	71	321	267
+15	+19	+88	+247
93	90	409	514

325 +261 = 6 / 86 / 586

43	84	477	699
+48	+17	+183	+128
91	101	660	827

Try these.

126	46	68	75	37	765	575
+352	+33	+21	+25	+57	+476	+426
478	79	89	100	94	1241	1001

311	132	631
+467	+225	+324
778	357	955

Addition Facts Complete these addition facts and sail your way to the next page.

32+88=120	31+79=110	15+98=113	33+97=130	85+69=154
39+84=123	89+58=147	24+96=120	85+97=182	82+48=130
43+67=110	49+94=143	51+69=120	95+99=194	91+87=178

Addition with regrouping

When the sum in any column is greater than 9, we need to regroup that number.

134

Hint: Be sure to keep the numbers lined up in the right place value column.

35

Addition, Two Minute Tornadoes - Page 6

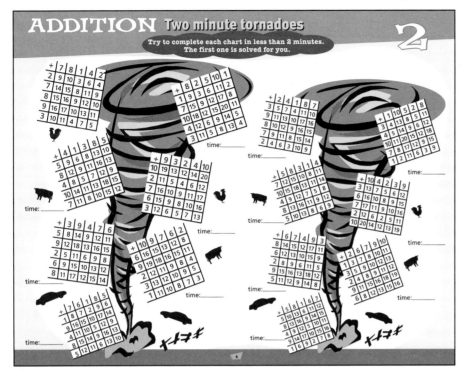

Subtraction 1 - Page 8

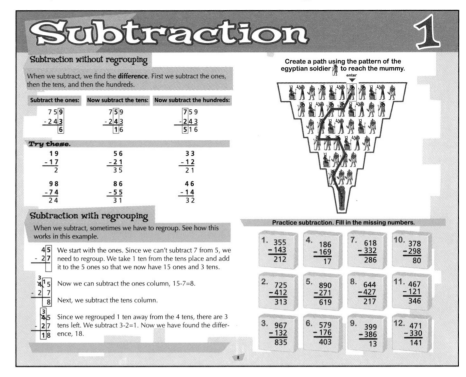

Addition, Secret Message - Page 7

Subtraction 2 - Page 9

Subtraction

Fact Families: Addition and Subtraction
Every addition fact has a related subtraction fact. These are called fact families. Knowing one fact helps you know the other facts in the family. Look at this array as an example.

The fact family for this array is:
6+3=9
3+6=9
9-3=6
9-6=3

Use each array to complete the fact family beside it.

1.
3 + 5 = 8
5 + 3 = 8
8 - 3 = 5
8 - 5 = 3

6.
7 +21=28
21 + 7 =28
28 - 7 =21
28-21= 7

2.
5 + 5 =10
5 + 5 =10
10 - 5 = 5
10 - 5 = 5

7.
8 +32=40
32+ 8 =40
40-32= 8
40- 8 =32

3.
2 + 6 = 8
6 + 2 = 8
8 - 2 = 6
8 - 6 = 2

4.
3 + 3 = 6
3 + 3 = 6
6 - 3 = 3
6 - 3 = 3

8.
11+ 9 = 20
9 +11=20
20- 9 =11
20-11= 9

5.
7 + 7 =14
7 + 7 =14
14 - 7 = 7
14 - 7 = 7

**Subtraction practice.
Fill in the missing numbers.**

1. 9 2
   - 6 1
     3 1

6. 9 6
   - 5 8
     3 8

11. 8 0
   - 5 4
     2 6

16. 2 1
   - 1 7
      4

2. 1 0 5
   - 7 1
      3 4

7. 7 4
   - 2 2
     5 2

12. 2 2
   - 2 0
      2

17. 8 0
   - 4 7
     3 3

3. 1 9 0
   - 7 5
    1 1 5

8. 1 4
   - 1 1
      3

13. 5 0
   - 1 6
     3 4

18. 9 8
   - 1 4
     8 4

4. 1 0 0
   - 6 9
      3 1

9. 4 7
   - 3 8
      9

14. 6 2
   - 4 5
     1 7

19. 5 8
   - 5 6
      2

5. 3 2
   - 2 5
      7

10. 7 6
   - 5 1
     2 5

15. 8 3
   - 3 5
     4 8

20. 9 6
   - 6 0
     3 6

Multiplication 1 - Page 10

Division 1 - Page 12

Multiplication 1 - Page 11

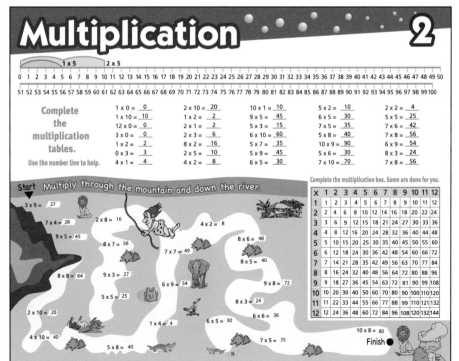

Division 2 - Page 13

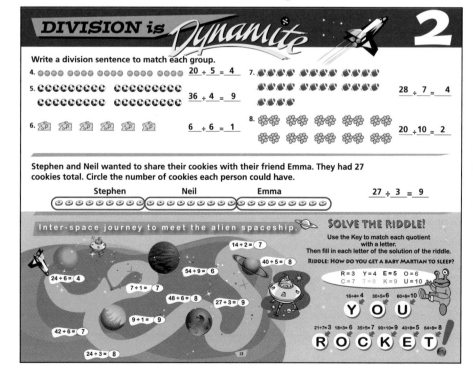

Graphs - Page 14

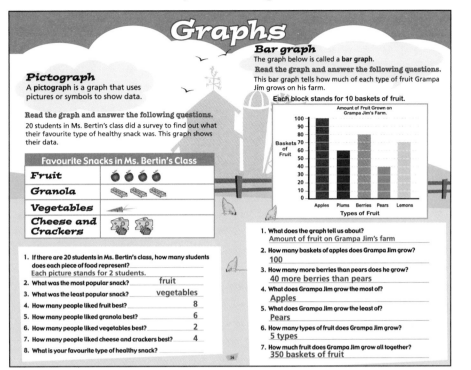

Graphs

Pictograph
A **pictograph** is a graph that uses pictures or symbols to show data.

Read the graph and answer the following questions.
20 students in Ms. Bertin's class did a survey to find out what their favourite type of healthy snack was. This graph shows their data.

Favourite Snacks in Ms. Bertin's Class

Fruit	
Granola	
Vegetables	
Cheese and Crackers	

1. If there are 20 students in Ms. Bertin's class, how many students does each piece of food represent?
Each picture stands for 2 students.
2. What was the most popular snack? fruit
3. What was the least popular snack? vegetables
4. How many people liked fruit best? 8
5. How many people liked granola best? 6
6. How many people liked vegetables best? 2
7. How many people liked cheese and crackers best? 4
8. What is your favourite type of healthy snack?

Bar graph
The graph below is called a **bar graph**.

Read the graph and answer the following questions.
This bar graph tells how much of each type of fruit Grampa Jim grows on his farm.

Each block stands for 10 baskets of fruit.

1. What does the graph tell us about?
Amount of fruit on Grampa Jim's farm
2. How many baskets of apples does Grampa Jim grow?
100
3. How many more berries than pears does he grow?
40 more berries than pears
4. What does Grampa Jim grow the most of?
Apples
5. What does Grampa Jim grow the least of?
Pears
6. How many types of fruit does Grampa Jim grow?
5 types
7. How much fruit does Grampa Jim grow all together?
350 baskets of fruit

Time - Page 15

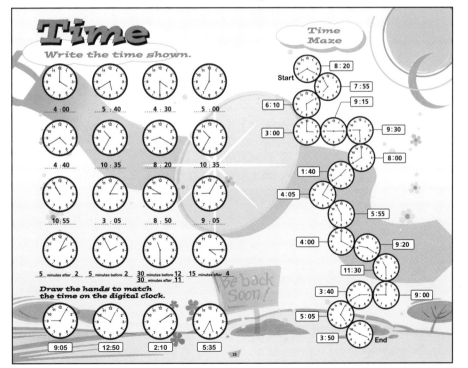

Time
Write the time shown.

4:00 | 5:40 | 4:30 | 5:00
4:40 | 10:35 | 8:20 | 10:35
10:55 | 3:05 | 8:50 | 9:05

5 minutes after 2 | 5 minutes before 2 | 30 minutes before 12 | 15 minutes after 4
| | 30 minutes after 11 |

Draw the hands to match the time on the digital clock.

9:05 | 12:50 | 2:10 | 5:35

Time Maze

Start
8:20
7:55
9:15
6:10
3:00
9:30
8:00
1:40
4:05
5:55
4:00
9:20
11:30
3:40
9:00
5:05
3:50
End

Fractions - Page 16

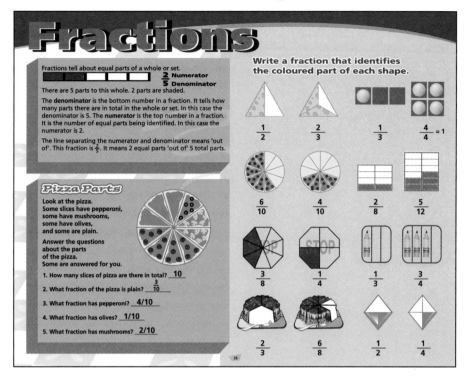

Fractions

Fractions tell about equal parts of a whole or set.
2 Numerator
5 Denominator
There are 5 parts to this whole. 2 parts are shaded.
The **denominator** is the bottom number in a fraction. It tells how many parts there are in total in the whole or set. In this case the denominator is 5. The **numerator** is the top number in a fraction. It is the number of equal parts being identified. In this case the numerator is 2.
The line separating the numerator and denominator means 'out of'. This fraction is $\frac{2}{5}$. It means 2 equal parts 'out of' 5 total parts.

Pizza Parts
Look at the pizza.
Some slices have pepperoni, some have mushrooms, some have olives, and some are plain.
Answer the questions about the parts of the pizza.
Some are answered for you.

1. How many slices of pizza are there in total? 10
2. What fraction of the pizza is plain? 3/10
3. What fraction has pepperoni? 4/10
4. What fraction has olives? 1/10
5. What fraction has mushrooms? 2/10

Write a fraction that identifies the coloured part of each shape.

$\frac{1}{2}$ | $\frac{2}{3}$ | $\frac{1}{3}$ | $\frac{4}{4} = 1$

$\frac{6}{10}$ | $\frac{4}{10}$ | $\frac{2}{8}$ | $\frac{5}{12}$

$\frac{3}{8}$ | $\frac{1}{4}$ | $\frac{1}{3}$ | $\frac{3}{4}$

$\frac{2}{3}$ | $\frac{6}{8}$ | $\frac{1}{2}$ | $\frac{1}{4}$

Money - Page 17

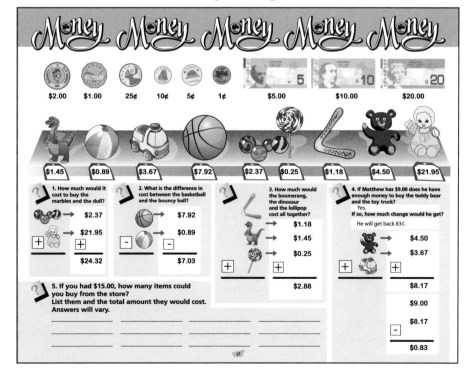

Money Money Money Money Money

$2.00 | $1.00 | 25¢ | 10¢ | 5¢ | 1¢ | $5.00 | $10.00 | $20.00

$1.45 | $0.89 | $3.67 | $7.92 | $2.37 | $0.25 | $1.18 | $4.50 | $21.95

1. How much would it cost to buy the marbles and the doll?
$2.37
+ $21.95
$24.32

2. What is the difference in cost between the basketball and the bouncy ball?
$7.92
− $0.89
$7.03

3. How much would the boomerang, the dinosaur and the lollipop cost all together?
$1.18
$1.45
+ $0.25
$2.88

4. If Matthew has $9.00 does he have enough money to buy the teddy bear and the toy truck?
Yes.
If so, how much change would he get?
He will get back 83¢.
$4.50
+ $3.67
$8.17
$9.00
− $8.17
$0.83

5. If you had $15.00, how many items could you buy from the store?
List them and the total amount they would cost.
Answers will vary.

Picture Dictionary - Page 20

Picture Dictionary

A picture dictionary is used to help understand the meaning of words and to find out how they are spelled. It is especially useful for defining nouns.

Look at the examples below. Think of another word for each letter. Draw a picture and write the word.

Ss	Tt	Uu	Vv	Ww	Xx	Yy	Zz
suitcase	teacher	umbrella	vacuum	whale	xylophone	yellow	zipper

Aa Bb Cc Dd Ee Ff Gg Hh Ii Jj Kk Ll Mm Nn Oo Pp Qq Rr Ss Tt Uu Vv Ww Xx Yy Zz

Solve the secret code. Write the letter beneath the symbol, then spell the word.

f i s h

d i n n e r

s p a c e s h i p

p u m p k i n

C a n a d a

C a l g a r y

T o r o n t o

O t t a w a

V a n c o u v e r

O n t a r i o

Q u e b e c

M a n i t o b a

N e w

B r u n s w i c k

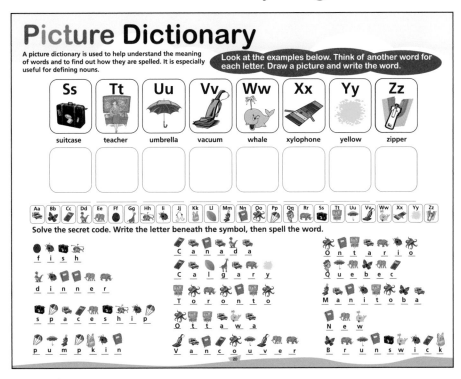

Ready for Action Verbs - Page 24

Ready for... ACTION VERBS!

Verbs

Remember: **Verbs** are **action words** like *shout, run, think, shine, hop, lick,* and also **being words** (called linking verbs) like *am, is, are.* There are also **helping verbs** that **help the main verb** tell about the action like *can wink, may leave, must ask.* All sentences need verbs.

Tickle the baby on the foot. (doing verb)

The sweater **is** fuzzy. (being verb)

When you **are** lost, you **must yell** for help. (being verb + helping verb + action verb)

Match the Present Tense.

I **bake** cookies. — wish

loves — play

I **wish** for a warm day. — My dog **loves** me.

I **play** in the backyard. — bake

Past Tense

We often use verbs in the past tense. They tell us what happened in the past.
*This morning I **got** dressed, **ate** breakfast, **brushed** my teeth, and then **rode** my bike to the park.*
*In olden times, people **travelled** by horse and buggy.*
*After our long hike this morning, we **were** tired.*

Past Tense Crossword Puzzle

Complete the puzzle with the past tense of each verb. The first one is done for you.

Across:	Down:
1. talk __talked__	5. eat __ate__
2. see __saw__	6. listen __listened__
3. open __opened__	7. write __wrote__
4. are __were__	8. do __did__

Tired Verbs and Vivid Verbs

Some verbs, like *said* and *went,* get used a lot. They can make a sentence sound tired. You can wake up tired sentences by using more vivid verbs.

Tired Verb: said

Vivid Verbs: Think of other vivid verbs:
whispered _____
croaked _____
giggled _____
moaned _____
cheered _____
hissed _____
bellowed _____

Write a vivid verb in sentence below. Use the list or think of your own.
"It's time to come home!" _____ the mother.
"We won," _____ the hockey player.
"Your costume is funny," _____ the boy.
The singer _____, "My throat hurts."
"I am finished my homework," _____ Anna.
"Shhh, _____ the librarian.

Tired Verb: went

Vivid Verbs: Think of other vivid verbs:
skipped _____
shuffled _____
raced _____
strode _____
marched _____
scampered _____
hopped _____
limped _____

Write a vivid verb in sentence below. Use the list or think of your own.
We _____ all the way around the track.
The children _____ to the park.
The monkeys _____ up the tree.
The tired runner _____ home to rest.
A mouse _____ across the floor.

Statements - Page 22

Grammar

Statements and Questions

Statements are sentences that tell information. They always start with a capital and end in a period.

Question sentences are asking for information. They always start with capital and end with a question mark (?). Many of them begin with asking words like *Who, Do, Did, How, What, Where, Why.*

Complete the final punctuation.
1. How old are you __?__
2. I like to eat chocolate ice cream __.__
3. My favourite food is pizza __.__
4. What did you do on your vacation __?__
5. How fast did you run __?__
6. My dog can play catch with me __.__
7. I got an A on my last math test __.__
8. Does your teacher give you homework __?__
9. The weather today is sunny and bright __.__
10. I want to have a fish for a pet __.__
11. Who is your best friend __?__
12. My friend Mei Lei and I like to play soccer __.__

Imagine you went to a birthday party.
Make up 2 of your own statement sentences about the party.
1. _____
2. _____

Make up 2 questions your mother or father might ask you about the party.
1. _____
2. _____

Nouns

A **common noun** is a person, place or thing.

Read the following passage and underline the nouns.
Yesterday I went to the <u>store</u> with my <u>friend</u> <u>Rashida</u>. We both wanted to buy some <u>candy</u>. We counted all of our <u>coins</u> and decided to buy some <u>candy fish</u>, a <u>chocolate bar</u> and a <u>bag of chips</u>. <u>Rashida</u> and I decided to share our <u>treats</u> while she walked her <u>dog</u>. She told me her <u>dog's</u> <u>name</u> was <u>Shadow</u>.

Place each noun you have underlined in the box it matches.

Person	Place	Thing
friend	store	candy
Rashida		coins
dog		candy fish
		chocolate bar
		bag of chips
		treats
		dog
		name
		Shadow

Proper Nouns

Proper nouns are nouns that name a specific person, place or thing. Proper nouns always start with capital letters.
Example:
common noun – boy, city, holiday
proper nouns – Omed, Ottawa, Christmas

Put the following nouns in the correct box. Be sure to capitalize the proper nouns.

thanksgiving, uncle, student, niagara falls, children, girl, barbara, school, c.n. tower, pencil | china, brother, sister, tuesday, ontario, city, ms. bertin, florida, cook, dr. landry | book, july, parent, library, calgary, camp, parking lot, dog

Common Nouns
uncle	school	city	library
student	pencil	cook	camp
children	brother	book	parking lot
girl	sister	parent	dog

Proper Nouns
Thanksgiving	Tuesday	July
Niagara Falls	Ontario	Monday
Barbara	Ms. Bertin	Calgary
C.N. Tower	Florida	
China	Dr. Landry	

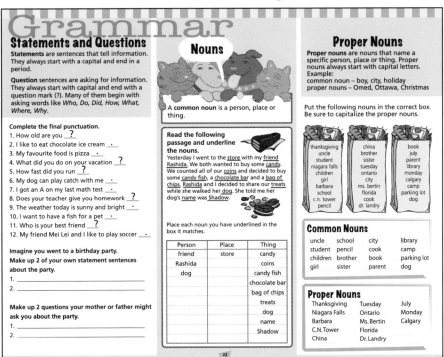

Adverbs - Page 25

Adverbs How~When~Where~How Much

How? When? Where? How much?

Adverbs always tell more about (or modify) verbs, adjectives, and even other adverbs. They always tell us *how, when, where,* or *how much.* Many adverbs end in *ly.*

How
I carefully walked around the broken glass.
How did I walk? **Carefully.**
The duck swam lazily across the pond.
How did the duck swim? **Lazily.**

When
He promptly returned the library book.
When did he return the library book? **Promptly.**
My brother practices the piano daily.
When does he practice? **Daily.**

Where
Wait here while I get my coat.
Wait where? **Here.**
Water sprayed everywhere when the wet dog shook himself.
Sprayed where? **Everywhere.**

How much
I am so happy with my new puppy.
How happy am I? **So happy.**
You are very tall.
How tall? **Very tall.**

How?
When?
Where?
How much?

Find each of the adverbs!

How adverbs
skillfully
sloppily
carefully
quickly
slowly
gently
roughly
crossly

When adverbs
never
always
yesterday
now
often
today
last
rarely

Where adverbs
here
there
away

How much adverbs
so
very
extremely
nearly
completely
totally
partially

Adverb Word Search

g	e	n	t	l	y			t	s	o
s	r			h	n		s	h	k	
l	o				e		l	e	i	p
o	u	o	c	n	v	a	o	r	l	a
w	g	f	a	e	e	l	p	e	l	r
l	h	t	r	a	r	w	p		f	t
y	l	e	e	r		a	i		u	i
	y	n	f	l	y	l	l		l	a
		u	y		s	y		l	l	l
l	a		l	h	e	r	e		y	l
a	w	l		c	r	o	s	s	l	y
s	a		y	q	u	i	c	k	l	y
t	y			s			t	o	d	a	y
y	e	s	t	e	r	d	a	y		
	r	a	r	e	l	y		y	r	
e	x	t	r	e	m	e	l	y		
l	c	o	m	p	l	e	t	e	l	y
t	o	t	a	l	l	y	v	e	r	y

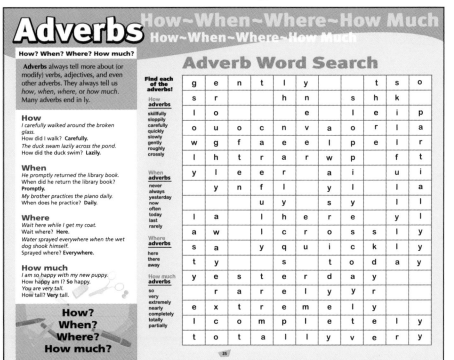